FROZEN TERROR

AS TOLD TO BEN EAST

ILLUSTRATED & DESIGNED
BY JACK DAHL

EDITED
BY JEROLYN NENTL
AND DR. HOWARD SCHROEDER

Professor in Reading and Language Arts, Dept. of Elementary Education, Mankato State University

Library of Congress Cataloging in Publication Data

East, Ben.
  Frozen terror.
  (Survival)
  SUMMARY— A man is stranded on an ice floe in Lake Michigan while ice fishing and endures perilous adventures attempting to get back to shore.
  1. Ice fishing--Michigan, Lake--Juvenile literature. 2. Wilderness survival--Juvenile literature. 3. Ice on rivers, lakes, etc.--Michigan, Lake--Juvenile literature. (1. Survival. 2. Michigan, Lake. 3. Ice on rivers, lakes, etc.) I. Dahl, John I. II. Nentl, Jerolyn Ann. III. Schroeder, Howard. IV. Title. V. Series.
SH455.45.E27   977.4   79-53747
ISBN 0-89686-049-3 lib. bdg.
ISBN 0-89686-057-4 pbk.

International Standard Book Numbers: **Library of Congress**
0-89686-049-3 Library Bound   **Catalog Number:**
0-89686-057-4 Paperback   79-53747

Adapted from the original publication *Narrow Escapes* by **Outdoor Life,** Copyright 1960.

CRESTWOOD HOUSE

P.O. Box 3427
Hwy. 66 South
Mankato, MN 56001

ABOUT THE AUTHOR...

Ben East has been an *Outdoor Life* staff editor since 1946. Born in south-eastern Michigan in 1898, and a lifelong resident of that state, he sold his first story to *Outers Recreation* (later absorbed by *Outdoor Life*) in 1921. In 1926 he began a career as a professional writer, becoming outdoor editor of Booth Newspapers, a chain of dailies in eight major Michigan cities outside Detroit.

He left the newspaper job on January 1, 1946, to become Midwest field editor of Outdoor Life. In 1966 he was advanced to senior field editor, a post from which he retired at the end of 1970. Since then he has continued to write for the magazine as a contributing field editor.

Growing up as a farm boy, he began fishing and hunting as soon as he could handle a cane pole and a .22 rifle. He has devoted sixty years to outdoor sports, travel, adventure, wildlife photography, writing and lecturing. Ben has covered much of the back country of North America, from the eastern seaboard to the Aleutian Islands of Alaska, and from the Canadian arctic to the southern United States. He has written more than one thousand magazine articles and eight books. Today his by-line is one of the best known of any outdoor writer in the country. His outstanding achievement in wildlife photography was the making of the first color film ever taken of the Alaskan sea otter, in the summer of 1941.

In recent years much of his writing has dealt with major conservation problems confronting the nation. He has produced hard-hitting and effective articles on such environmentally destructive practices as strip mining, channelization, unethical use of aircraft to take trophy game, political interference in wildlife affairs, the indiscriminate use of pesticides and the damming of wild and scenic rivers and streams.

In 1973, he was signally honored when the Michigan Senate and House of Representatives adopted a concurrent resolution, the legislature's highest tribute, recognizing him for his distinguished contribution to the conservation of natural resources.

A FOREWORD TO FROZEN TERROR

This is a true story. It is hard to believe that a man could endure all that Lewis Sweet went through during that terrible week in January and live to tell about it.

I took part in the search for the lost fisherman on the final day an attempt was made to find him. I was one of the three men who walked the rough shore ice around Waugoshance Point looking for Sweet on the Sunday he walked and crawled from White Shoals lighthouse to the mainland. Had we carried binoculars (for which we thought there was no need), we would have seen the small, black figure creeping across the ice fields. Sweet would then have been rescued two days before he finally came ashore at Cross Village.

I got to know him well after he was released from the hospital. At that time I was living in Grand Rapids, Michigan. The owner of a theater there engaged Sweet as a feature of his nightly show. Lewis Sweet was brought onto the stage in a wheelchair. There he told his story to a packed theater each night for a week.

I spent much time with him in his hotel room that week. At that time we went over every detail of his story. There is no doubt that every word of it is true.

I have known many men who showed great courage in the face of danger. None have been more steadfast than this northern Michigan fisherman. Against odds that would have caused many to give up, he fought on and refused to die.

His story, as it is told here, is one of the stirring sagas of the Great Lakes.

BEN EAST

It was a bitterly cold Tuesday in the middle of January. Lewis Sweet and two friends had hiked across the snowy, rocky beach of Crane Island at the north end of Lake Michigan. Then they climbed over the rough shore ice and headed for the open waters of the huge lake. A mile off shore, each man had a darkhouse. A darkhouse is a small lightproof shelter used for ice fishing.

The men kept small stoves in their darkhouses for heat. Sweet quickly lit a fire after he arrived. The warmth felt good. Then he tied a wooden minnow onto the end of his line, and dropped it into the water.

LEWIS SWEET
ALANSON, MICH.

There was no hint this day would be different from any other Sweet had spent ice fishing. He wanted to catch four or five trout by late afternoon, then head back to shore. It was a thirty mile drive to the village of Alanson where he lived.

The men were on the northwest tip of Michigan's lower peninsula, west of Waugoshance Point. The point was a long, narrow strip of sand running out into the lake. It had few trees, no roads, and was very wild. There was no one living on the island or the point. Ice fishing from the point was very good.

Sweet waited a long time in his darkhouse for the first trout to show up. He was a very patient man. Perhaps that was why he liked ice fishing so much. Each time he saw a fish under the ice, Sweet drove his spear down hard. The handle of the spear was a steel rod eight feet long. It was tied to the roof of the darkhouse by fifty feet of rope. When he felt the head of the spear go deep into the fish, he let go of the handle. The weight of the spear carried the fish toward the bottom. Once the fish stopped struggling, he pulled it up by the rope. There was not much room in the darkhouse, so he had to back out the door to take each fish off the spear.

Sweet was sitting in his darkhouse, waiting for another trout, when he heard a noise outside.

9

His two friends had quit fishing and walked across the ice to his darkhouse. Sweet had been so busy fishing, he had not noticed that the wind was getting stronger. The air was now full of snow. It had turned out to be a blustery day. It was the kind of weather that ice fishermen must watch closely.

Sweet looked out the door and squinted at the sky. "We're going back, Lew," a voice called to him. "The wind is changing to the northeast. It doesn't look good. Better come along."

"It'll be okay for awhile, I guess," he told them. "The ice will hold unless the wind gets stronger. I want just one more fish." Having said that, Sweet shut the door. Earlier that morning the wind had been blowing from the west, toward land. Had it kept blowing from that direction there would have been nothing to worry about.

His friends walked toward shore, leaving Sweet alone on the ice. He continued to fish but promised to check the wind often. Only a half hour had gone by when he was startled by a sudden noise. He listened carefully. A low rumble came from the east. It was a grinding, groaning noise which ran across the ice field like rolling thunder. The little darkhouse shook as if a train had passed.

Sweet knew the noise could mean only one thing. He grabbed his ax and the trout he had speared and ran from the darkhouse. There was no

11

time to lose. He ran as fast as he could toward Crane Island. As he got closer to the beach, he saw a narrow, black line running across the white ice. It was what he had feared most. The ice he was on was breaking off from the island. The narrow black line was the widening gap of water. He was being pushed out into Lake Michigan by the wind!

If Sweet could get to the crack before it got too wide, he would be able to jump across. He ran as fast as he could. The crack was ten feet across when he reached it, and was getting wider with each second. He did not dare jump now. It would be too big a chance to take. If he did not make it, he would freeze to death in the icy waters. There would also be a sucking undertow from the many tons of ice being pushed out into the lake by the wind. Even if he could stand the cold and undertow, Sweet figured he would not be able to crawl up the other side of the ice. It would be too smooth and slick.

The gap of water grew from ten to twenty feet, and then to one hundred feet. Soon Sweet could barely see land. He turned around and sadly walked back to his darkhouse. He had enough firewood to last through the night so he would be cozy and warm. Yet Sweet knew he could not allow himself that comfort. His only chance for keeping himself alive was to stay out in the open. He would have to watch the ice for cracks. The ice field would be breaking up as the wind blew it out into the lake. Sweet would have to stay on the main chunk. It would mean certain death to get caught on one of the smaller pieces breaking off from the main floe. The main floe was about three miles wide, but only two feet thick.

Sweet turned from the darkhouse and walked away. He walked to the center of the drifting ice floe and began building a low wall of snow. The wall would give him some shelter from the wind. This was hard, slow, work and his only tool was an ax. He had not been working very long when a sharp crack ripped across the ice. Looking up he saw his darkhouse settling into the water. As he watched, the smaller piece of ice crunched back against the main ice field. The darkhouse broke into small pieces as if it had been made of cardboard. Sweet felt helpless! A half hour later the darkhouses of his two friends met the same fate. His last hope of shelter was gone. Whatever happened now, Sweet would have to see it through on the open ice. There would be nothing between him and the cold wind but the snow wall.

Sweet knew what he faced. There was no way he could know his chances of survival. The ice field might go aground on one of the islands. If it did, he would be rescued or walk to safety. If it did not,

15

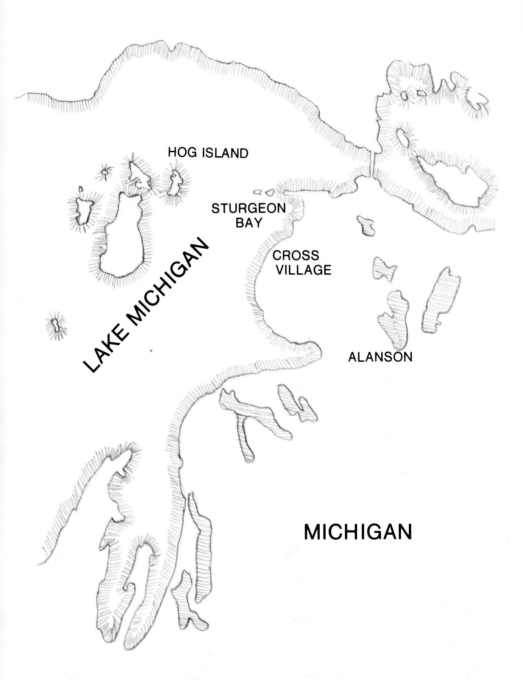

HOG ISLAND

STURGEON
BAY

CROSS
VILLAGE

LAKE MICHIGAN

ALANSON

MICHIGAN

16

there were sixty miles of open water between him and the west shore of the lake. Sweet knew the ice floe might not hold together that long in a winter storm. Even if it did, there was little chance of a steady wind. Only a steady wind would drive the floe straight across the lake. By morning he was afraid the wind would be blowing from the northeast. His ice floe would be out in the middle of the lake by then, beyond the islands. With a northeast wind behind him, he could drift more than one hundred miles across the lake without seeing land!

Suddenly, Sweet stopped daydreaming. Straight ahead, right in the path of his ice floe, was Waugoshance Lighthouse. He was headed straight for it! It looked as though the floe would go aground right at the foot of the light!

Since the lighthouse was not being used, there would be no fuel or food there. It was only a shell of rusted steel, with no windows, sitting on a pile of rock and concrete. Yet it was a pinpoint of solid ground out in the huge lake. It would be shelter from the wind and the icy waters. It meant survival, at least for awhile.

Hope swelled in Sweet's heart. It was midafternoon, and the early darkness of winter would soon be settling over the lake. He watched the lighthouse with eager eyes as he got closer and closer. Then, with no warning, the lake currents shifted. It was a slight shift, but enough to change the direction of the ice floe. It slid past the lighthouse, missing it by only a hundred yards. Sweet could not believe his eyes. There was nothing he could do as he watched the tower fade out of sight. He was again headed for the open waters of the lake.

Meanwhile, search and rescue teams were being called to look for Sweet. His two friends had still been on Crane Island when they heard the ice break. They were worried about Sweet, so waited for him to come back to the beach. Through the

blinding snow, they had seen the black crack of open water. They knew he was still out there on the ice. The men jumped into their car and headed for Cross Village, high on the bluffs of Sturgeon Bay ten miles to the south.

When they got there, word of Lewis Sweet's plight spread quickly. Was he still alive? It was an old theme: man against the weather. Sweet was small and helpless against the endless waste of ice and water, wind and snow.

There was not much that could be done the first twenty-four hours. No search attempt could begin in a blinding snowstorm. All anyone could do was wait and hope for the best. By Wednesday noon, the storm had blown itself out. A full search and rescue operation was underway by nightfall. There was too much ice in the north end of the lake for boats. The search had to be made from the air and on foot. Volunteers searched the frozen shores of Waugoshance Point, Crane Island and around Sturgeon Bay. They searched the islands that lay farther out in the lake, too. For four days, they joined forces with Coast Guard crews to check the beaches. They watched for tracks, a thread of smoke, or a dead fire, any sign at all that Sweet had made it back to the mainland. Pilots flew over two thousand square miles of lake and ice looking for a man huddled on a drifting ice floe or on one of the islands.

The searchers did all they could. Although three days passed, no trace of Sweet had been found. Little by little, hour by hour, hope dimmed among the volunteers. It seemed as though time had run out. By Friday night, all hope was gone. They assumed no one could survive so many hours of cold and stormy weather without food and shelter.

Saturday was the fourth and last day of the search. The volunteers, who showed up that day, looked only for a dark spot on a beach that might be Sweet's body. By dark, even hope of finding his body dimmed. The search ended. Not many wondered whether or not Lewis Sweet would be rescued. Few wondered how. They could only guess where his body might be found, or if it would ever be found.

But, Lewis Sweet had not died!

He had almost ended his adventure the same afternoon he went adrift. Twice more after Waugoshance Lighthouse, Sweet thought he was going aground. The first time it was on Hat Island, the second time was Hog Island.

Through the storm Sweet thought he could see Hat Island. At first it looked like just a dot on the churning water. The air was full of snow and it was hard to see. His ice floe seemed to be going straight toward the island. Sweet was sure it would go aground on the beach. He knew no one lived on Hat Island. Even though there would be no shelter on the island, anything would be warmer than the ice floe. The island was wooded, so there would be plenty of dry wood to build a fire. Using the trout he had caught, Sweet would have food. He thought that staying warm and eating would keep him alive long enough to be rescued. Excitement flowed through his body! It was great to know he would not die out on the lake!

Sweet was thinking how good it would feel to trade his drifting ice floe for solid ground when the wind had again shifted. The course of his ice floe was changing. The wind was pushing him past the island, just as it had done at Waugoshance Point. The ice floe was drifting farther and farther out into the huge lake.

23

Soon the ice floe came close to another island. This time Sweet did not get his hopes up so high. Hog Island lay ahead. It was a much bigger island, but also without shelter. A seagull flew from the rough shore ice and landed next to Sweet. Then it flew back leaving Sweet wishing that he, too, could fly. Again, the wind and the lake currents played their tricks, and the ice floe drifted past the island just a few yards from the beach.

Tuesday night was rough. Sweet was out in the open water now, miles from any land. There was nothing to keep the winter storm from dumping its full fury on the thin floe of ice. The storm soon became a raging blizzard. Sweet tried not to lose faith. By now darkness covered the lake and he knew the worst was yet to come.

Suddenly the ice, where Sweet had built his snow shelter, broke from the main floe! There was no warning. Sweet heard a splintering noise and saw the crack starting to widen only a few yards away. Picking up his fish as fast as he could, he grabbed the ax and ran. There was one place where the pressure of the wind still held the two pieces of ice together. Sweet raced toward that spot as fast as he could. He jumped. Although the crack had widened to several feet, he made it across to the main floe.

Sweet breathed a sigh of relief and went to work building another snow shelter. The work kept him from worrying. He lay down behind the shelter as soon as it was done, but the cold numbed him after only a few minutes. Jumping to his feet, he started running back and forth across the ice. Sweet had to get his blood flowing again to warm his body. As he ran, the wind-driven snow cut his face like a whip. Once he was warm, he lay down, but again the cold numbed him. For a second time, Sweet got up and raced across the ice. All night, he rested only in short spurts. He would lie down awhile behind the snow wall, then get up and run. To sleep would mean freezing to death.

The ice floe broke in two again just before midnight. Sometime in the early hours of morning, it broke a third time. Both times, Sweet had to again abandon his snow shelter so that he could stay on the main ice floe. Both times he was lucky. He had just enough time to grab his trout and his ax.

Toward daybreak the wind played tricks again. It shifted to the southwest, reversing the drift of the ice. The wind was now blowing his ice floe back the way from which it had come. An hour before dawn, with no warning, it went aground! The sudden crunching sound was like thunder. Directly in front of Sweet the edge of the ice rose out of the water! It curled back on itself and came crashing down in a rain of two-ton blocks. The entire floe shook! It seemed about to splinter into a million pieces. Sweet ran away from the spot where it was going aground. It took almost ten minutes to finally come to rest! At last, the grinding noise ended.

The ice floe had stayed together better than Sweet had thought it would. It was still two miles wide, although it was full of cracks. He walked carefully in the predawn darkness to find out what had happened. Sweet had no idea where he was or what had stopped the ice floe. Exploring the jumble of ice chunks, he was surprised to find that it had gone aground at the foot of White Shoals Lighthouse. The tower rose from a crib built on an

underwater reef. Sweet's ice floe had slid aground on the reef. The heavy concrete crib holding the lighthouse had sliced into it like a giant snow plow.

Sweet knew shelter, food, and fuel for a fire awaited him at the top of the lighthouse. He would be safe there for awhile. His first job was to find a way to the top. It was twenty-two feet up the side to the lighthouse. To make things worse, the crib was encased in ice a foot thick! The steel ladder going up the side could only be seen as a bulge on the face of the ice.

Sweet gathered his strength and, in the soft gray light of that stormy winter morning, went to work with his ax. He chopped away at the ice as high as he could reach while still standing on the ice floe. Slowly, one at a time, the rungs of the ladder emerged. When he could reach no higher, he stood

on the first rung. He hung on with one hand while chopping with the other. It was slow work. For three hours, Sweet chipped away at the ice. At last, he was within three rungs of the top. Food, shelter, and warmth were less than a yard away.

Instead of feeling safe, Sweet lost hope. His hands had lost all feeling more than two hours ago. They were so badly frozen now that he could no longer keep a good grip on either the ladder or the ax. He had already dropped the ax half a dozen times, and been forced to climb down the ladder to get it. The first few times, climbing back up the rungs was not so bad. After that, the climb had gotten more and more difficult. His feet were like wooden stumps and it was impossible to feel his

30

weight on them. Each time he climbed a step Sweet had to look to make sure his fingers were hooked around a rung.

If the ax fell again, Sweet knew he would not be able to climb back up the ladder. Taking a few small strokes, the ax went clattering down, just as he knew it would. Sweet climbed stiffly down the ladder and huddled on a block of ice to rest. He thought of his family and friends, and his life back in Alanson.

Lewis Sweet did not want to die. It is hard to give up and die of cold and hunger when warmth and food are only a few feet away. There had to be some way to the top of that ice-coated crib. He was going to find it before the storm killed him!

An idea came to Sweet as he sat bent over on a piece of ice. He could build a ramp to the top of the crib out of ice chunks. The blocks were there waiting for him. They had piled up when the edge of the ice floe had shattered against the base of the lighthouse. Some of the blocks were so large that ten men could not have moved them, but many were small enough for Sweet to lift by himself. He went back to work.

His frozen fingers could barely grasp the slippery chunks of ice. Sweet kept working, and three hours later had the job finished. Slowly, he crawled and dragged himself up to the top of the crib. The lighthouse crew had left the door unlocked when they closed up for the winter. There was a heavy screen on it, but that was no problem for a man with an ax.

Finally, Sweet was inside the lighthouse! In all his fifty years he had never known a happier moment! There were bacon, rice, dried fruit, flour, tea and other supplies. He saw three small stoves and plenty of fuel and matches. It was all a man needed to live for days or weeks, maybe even until spring!

Sweet sat down in the midst of his treasures. Now that he was out of the weather Sweet only wanted to sleep. He had no interest in food and was just too tired to eat. He cut the shoes off his frozen feet. Then after having warmed his hands and feet over one of the stoves, he crawled into a bed and fell asleep.

Lewis Sweet was alone in a frozen lighthouse, one of the loneliest places on the lake. White Shoals Lighthouse was a concrete island. It was one hundred feet square, built in the middle of the lake. It had been closed since the end of the boating season. The nearest land was more than a dozen miles away, and a January blizzard was raging. Sweet's hands and feet were frozen, and no one had any idea where he was. No one even knew he was alive. It was not a good spot to be in, but it was better than drifting across the lake on a field of ice.

Sweet slept for almost twenty-four hours. When he awoke, he was hungry. He went through the food left in the lighthouse, and cooked the first meal he had eaten in two days. The food gave him new strength. He started thinking about his fate. The weather had cleared, and Sweet could see the shore of the lake both to the north and south. He could even see Crane Island where he had gone adrift. Between him and the land lay miles of icy water dotted with drifting ice floes. From the lighthouse, the lake looked like a huge white field laced with dark veins. It would take a night of severe cold without wind to freeze the open cracks. If the cracks did not freeze over, Sweet would never be able to leave the lighthouse on his own. He would become its prisoner. That would not have worried him had it not been for his frozen hands and feet. He knew they would have to be cared for by a doctor. He also knew the lake might not freeze over the rest of the winter. It was not a very happy thought, but Sweet decided he would not worry. He would take one thing at a time.

First he needed to find out what supplies were in the lighthouse. During the morning he sorted through everything he could find. After that, he sat down beside the stove to care for his feet. As he was caring for his blisters, a noise caught his attention. A hum was getting louder and louder. Instinct told him it was a rescue plane sent to search for him. Sweet jumped up on his crippled feet and hobbled to the nearest window. The windows were covered with heavy screen to protect them from the wind and the weather. There was no way to wave or signal from any of them. He went to the stairs. The door, through which he had entered the lighthouse, was several flights below the living quarters. There wasn't enough time for him to make it that far. His only chance was one flight up, in the lens room at the top of the tower. He knew there was another door there.

Sweet climbed the iron stairs as fast as his swollen feet would carry him, but he was too late. The plane was far out over the lake as he opened the door. It quickly disappeared in the south.

The pilot of the plane had gone out of his way to have a look at White Shoals Lighthouse. He thought Sweet might be there. Tipping his plane in a steep bank, the pilot roared around the lighthouse. Seeing nothing but a ridge of ice and snow, he leveled off and headed home to refuel.

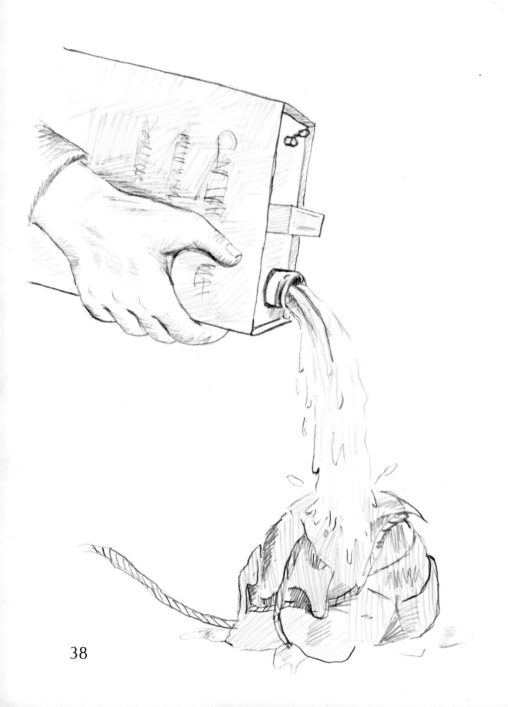

38

Most people would have lost heart at seeing the plane fly away. However, Sweet had been through too much to give up at that point. He headed back to the living quarters to continue giving first aid to his feet. Later in the day, another plane roared over White Shoals. This one didn't even circle the lighthouse. Sweet watched helplessly through a screened window while it flew out of sight. Seeing the second plane fly away convinced him. If he were to get home, he would have to do it on his own. He was sure that no one had figured out where he was. Since the lake was not frozen over, he would be unable to leave the lighthouse. What could he do?

Sweet decided he would try to signal the mainland. The big light would attract attention at that time of the year, but he could find no way to turn it on. Instead, he made a flare. Soaking rags in oil, he rolled them into a ball and tied it to the end of a long wire. That night, he went out on the balcony of the lens room. He lit the ball and swung it gently back and forth. It made only a small red flame, which he hoped might be seen by someone on shore. As Sweet swung his ball of fire, he could see the friendly lights of Cross Village. They twinkled from their high bluff twenty miles away. Oh, how close they seemed! He could almost feel the warmth from the cozy fires inside the homes.

No one from the village saw his signal, but Sweet did not give up easily. Friday morning he hung out flares just in case another plane might fly near the lighthouse. During the day he cooked three good meals, and continued looking after his feet. As new blisters appeared, he opened and cared for them. At dark, he climbed back up to the lens room and went outside. There was a bitter cold wind blowing. He lit his oil-soaked rag ball and swung it back and forth for a long time. Twice more during the night he sent his faint signal, but his efforts brought nothing. No one came to rescue him.

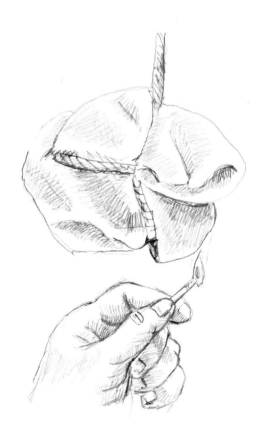

On Saturday, the lake was still open. He would have to remain on the reef. That night it was very still. The wind went down and the stars twinkled brightly. It was getting colder. Sweet began to think that he might be able to escape from the lighthouse after all. He went to bed that night renewed with hope. Awaking the next morning, he was overjoyed by what he saw. There were no open cracks of water in sight. Everything was covered with new ice as far as he could see. Sweet knew Lake Michigan well, and that the ice would hold up under a man's weight. There was no way he could know for sure if he would find open water before he reached the shore. It really didn't matter. Sweet knew he could not survive in the lighthouse much longer. His feet were in bad shape. In another day or two he would not be able to use them at all. He was sure the

42

search for him had been called off, and that if he did not get away from White Shoals Lighthouse now, he might never leave it alive. It was the first time the weather had given him a chance to get away, and he would have to take it.

How he was going to get across the miles of ice on his crippled feet, Sweet wasn't sure. His feet were too swollen for shoes. He could only wear socks. There had been plenty of heavy woolen socks in the lighthouse supplies. He pulled on four pairs, one over the next. Sweet wore his heavy rubbers over the socks. He would have to take it slow, one mile at a time.

Carefully, Sweet climbed down from the lighthouse, leaving behind shelter, food, and warmth. As he started across the ice, Sweet carried both his ax and the frozen trout. If he made it to the shore, he would need the ax to cut fire wood and the trout to eat. They had also become symbols of his fierce desire to stay alive.

About the same time, three men set out from Wilderness State Park, ten miles east of Crane Island. The search for Sweet had been called off, but these men wanted to have one last look. They snowshoed down the beach and searched the rough shore ice around the point. White Shoals Lighthouse looked like a far-off gray stick rising out of the frozen lake. Below it was Sweet, crawling at the speed of a snail across the ice. The three searchers could not see him. He was too far away. They searched the ice mounds on the shore near the point all day, looking for Sweet's body. That day, unknown to them, Lewis Sweet was creeping across the ice toward them.

Inside his heavy socks, Sweet could feel fresh blisters swelling on his feet. Taking a few steps, he would sit down to rest, and then get up and continue on. At times, he got down on his hands and knees and crawled.

Late Sunday afternoon, Sweet passed the tip of Crane Island at about the spot where he had gone adrift. It was almost dark, but he did not go ashore. His goal was Cross Village. It was the closest place where he could find help, and Sweet knew he could make better time on the open ice than on the rocky beach. It was getting harder for him to stay on course. He was getting very tired.

At dark, Sweet came upon a deserted shanty on the shore of the bay. Being seven miles from the village, the shanty would provide shelter for the night. In it there was firewood and a rusty stove. There was no food, only coffee and a frozen can of milk. He still had his trout, but was too weak to cook it. Using the last of his strength he built a fire. Sweet made some coffee and crawled to the bunk.

By morning he was both sick to his stomach and had bad cramps. He did not know if it was from the lack of food or from the frozen milk he had put in his coffee the night before. Trying to get up, Sweet found he was unable to stand. All that Monday he lay helpless in the shanty. He ate nothing.

By the time he awoke the next morning, he was feeling better. Sweet had gained a little strength from his rest, and was able to start out once more. He could not give up now; there were only a few miles left to go! Sweet hobbled and crawled over the rough ice of Sturgeon Bay all morning. It was almost noon by the time he reached the steep bluff leading up to the village. Climbing slowly up the bank, he called to a passing stranger. Then he collapsed, dropping his ax and frozen trout at last. Lewis Sweet had come home from the lake, alone and without help!

The stranger quickly got Sweet to a hospital. Doctors did their best, but were not able to save his frozen fingers and toes. All of them had to be removed. Sweet stayed in the hospital for ten weeks while his hands and feet slowly healed. It was quite a price to pay, but Lewis Sweet had lived to tell about his painful and unusual adventure. He had refused to give up!

Stay on the edge of your seat.

Read:

FROZEN TERROR

DANGER IN THE AIR

MISTAKEN JOURNEY

TRAPPED IN DEVIL'S HOLE

DESPERATE SEARCH

FORTY DAYS LOST

FOUND ALIVE

GRIZZLY!

SURVIVAL TRUE STORIES